Effective BOUNDARY Setting Workbook

A Practical Guide to Understanding Your Needs and Establishing Healthy Limits

Isabella Cruz

"Good fences make good neighbors." – Robert Frost

III

Acknowledgement

I'm incredibly grateful to Dr. Greg Stones for his invaluable guidance along the way.

A special thanks to Dr. Liam David for her constant encouragement that kept me moving forward.

I want to acknowledge the big contributions of Joel and Craig – I couldn't have done this without them.

And finally, my deepest gratitude goes to David and Bella for their endless love and support. Thank you for always being there.

About the Author

Isabella Cruz is a renowned psychologist and resilience coach, known for her empowering and relatable approach to mental health. Holding a doctorate in Psychology from Stanford University, she specializes in cognitive-behavioral therapy and mindfulness techniques.

With extensive experience in clinical practice, Isabella has dedicated her career to helping individuals overcome mental barriers and achieve emotional freedom. She lives in Seattle, where she continues to inspire and support others through her practice, coaching, and public speaking.

Other Books by this same author includes:

Table
Of Contents

How To Use This Workbook

Start with Self-Reflection: Find a quiet moment to look inward and think about your own experiences with attachment. Taking this time will help you feel more connected to what you're learning.

Read Each Chapter Carefully: Move through each chapter at your own pace, allowing yourself time to really understand the ideas and how they relate to you.

Complete the Exercises: Once you've read a section, dive into the exercises. These are meant to help you explore your feelings, thoughts, and behaviors around avoidant attachment.

Journal Your Thoughts: Use the provided space to jot down anything that stands out to you—your thoughts, insights, and any patterns you start to see as you work through each exercise.

Practice Consistently: Consistency is everything. Try to set aside regular time each week, even just a few minutes a day, to keep up with the exercises.

Reflect and Review: Now and then, look back at your notes and completed exercises. Take a moment to see how far you've come and how your understanding of avoidant attachment has shifted.

Apply What You Learn: Start using the insights and strategies in your daily life. Notice how things may begin to shift in your relationships and interactions.

Revisit as Needed: This workbook is here to support your growth. Don't hesitate to come back to sections that resonate or take on new meaning as your journey unfolds.

"You teach people how to treat you by what you allow, what you stop, and what you reinforce." – Tony Gaskins

Introduction

On an ordinary Monday morning, in the midst of India's fight for independence, Mahatma Gandhi did something quite unexpected—he chose not to speak. This wasn't a protest or a rebellion.

It was a personal ritual, one he followed every Monday, regardless of the urgent matters demanding his attention. Gandhi called it **Maun Vrat**, a vow of silence. It was one of the most profound boundaries he set for himself.

At a time when the country was engulfed in political unrest, and countless people relied on him for direction, Gandhi understood something critical: to lead effectively, he needed to create space for himself. So, every Monday, he went silent.

This wasn't just about taking a break; it was about protecting his mental, emotional, and spiritual well-being. People would approach him with pressing issues—matters related to India's future, the needs of the masses—but Gandhi remained steadfast.

He knew that without these moments of silence and reflection, he would lose the clarity that guided his nonviolent movement. For him, silence wasn't optional; it was essential.

During these quiet days, Gandhi grappled with difficult questions, about both himself and the world. It was a time for recharging, deep thinking, and meditating on the principles of truth *(Satya)* and nonviolence *(Ahimsa)* that underpinned his activism.

This stillness gave him the strength to continue leading a nation toward freedom, even in the face of enormous challenges. His Mondays weren't just about resting; they were about resetting. By respecting his need for silence, Gandhi showed the world how setting personal boundaries can help build resilience, spark insight, and allow us to show up more purposefully.

For many of us, the idea of taking a day for ourselves—especially during a crisis—might seem unthinkable or even selfish.

But Gandhi understood that boundaries don't block leadership; they sustain it. In protecting his space for quiet and reflection, he saved his energy for the battles that really mattered.

His silence didn't weaken him; it strengthened him. Through this, Gandhi taught us an important lesson we often overlook: when we don't set boundaries, we risk losing ourselves in the noise of the world.

Many of us today struggle with setting boundaries in our lives. We live in a world that constantly pulls at our attention—whether it's work, family, friends, or the endless buzz of social media.

We feel compelled to say yes, to be always available, and to keep going even when we're exhausted, believing that's what success, love, or responsibility demands.

But here's the reality: without clear boundaries, we deplete ourselves, lose focus on what truly matters, and diminish our ability to live a fulfilling, healthy life.

This workbook is here to help you, much like Gandhi, carve out those sacred spaces in your own life. It will walk you through understanding your personal needs, pinpointing where your boundaries are weak or missing, and give you practical tools to strengthen and maintain them.

Whether it's protecting your time, expressing your emotional needs, or setting limits in relationships, this workbook will help you take back control. In doing so, you'll realize that boundaries aren't about shutting others out—they're about staying true to yourself.

Just like Gandhi, when you respect your boundaries, you make room to show up as your best self. This isn't just about learning to say "no," but about recognizing when and where to say "yes" to the things that align with your values and goals. Through this workbook, you'll gain the clarity and confidence to prioritize what truly matters and build the life you deserve, one healthy boundary at a time.

In the upcoming chapters, you'll explore how to recognize your personal limits, communicate them clearly, and deal with the inevitable pushback when you start standing up for your needs.

You'll also discover the freedom that comes from protecting your own well-being, much like Gandhi safeguarded his time for reflection. Boundaries are your way of telling the world, ***"This is what I need to thrive."*** And when you honor them, you'll find the strength to navigate life with peace, purpose, and clarity.

Below's a quiz that you can take to test whether you have strong or weak boundary-setting skills. It includes simple "Yes" or "No" responses, with scoring guidelines at the end to determine how strong or weak your boundary-setting skills are.

I find it easy to say "no" to requests that don't align with my values or priorities.

- Yes
- No

I rarely feel guilty when I assert my personal boundaries with others.

- Yes
- No

When someone oversteps my boundaries, I feel comfortable addressing the issue directly.

- Yes
- No

I know the difference between being assertive and being aggressive when setting boundaries.

- Yes
- No

I can maintain my boundaries even when I care deeply about the person involved.

- Yes
- No

I don't allow others to manipulate or guilt-trip me into doing things I don't want to do.

- Yes
- No

I recognize when I'm feeling uncomfortable or resentful because my boundaries are being crossed.

- Yes
- No

I am consistent in enforcing my boundaries, even when faced with resistance.

- Yes
- No

I respect other people's boundaries and don't take it personally when they say "no."

- Yes
- No

I feel empowered and in control of my life when I set and maintain boundaries.

- Yes
- No

Scoring:

For each "Yes," give yourself 1 point.
For each "No," give yourself 0 points.

Results:

8-10 Points: Strong Boundary-Setting Skills

You have a solid understanding of boundaries and know how to assert them effectively. You respect your own needs and the boundaries of others, which allows you to maintain healthy relationships without feeling drained or resentful.

5-7 Points: Moderate Boundary-Setting Skills

You generally do well at setting boundaries, but there may be a few areas where you struggle, especially when it comes to maintaining them under pressure. You may need to practice consistency or work on specific situations where boundaries are harder to uphold.

0-4 Points: Weak Boundary-Setting Skills

You may have difficulty setting or enforcing boundaries, leading to feelings of overwhelm, guilt, or resentment. It might be helpful to work on building confidence and communication skills to better assert your needs.

Chapter 1

THE POWER OF BOUNDARIES

One of the most significant studies on the psychological impact of boundaries was led by **Dr. Henry Cloud and Dr. John Townsend**, both respected psychologists and authors of the influential book Boundaries: ***When to Say Yes, How to Say No to Take Control of Your Life, published in 1992.***

While the book itself gained widespread acclaim, it was grounded in years of clinical research and therapy sessions, primarily conducted in California, where both psychologists worked in private practice.

Through their research, Cloud and Townsend examined the consequences of lacking clear boundaries, revealing links to burnout, depression, and feelings of resentment.

They analyzed patterns in the lives of hundreds of clients, finding that those who struggled to establish boundaries often faced emotional exhaustion, strained relationships, and a diminished sense of autonomy.

Over time, they discovered a direct correlation between weak boundaries and difficulty managing stress effectively.

One of their pivotal findings highlighted the impact of boundaries on emotional well-being. When individuals feel unable to say no, their sense of personal agency begins to erode.

This often leads to a ***"compliance trap,"*** where people feel compelled to meet others' expectations, often at the expense of their own needs. In contrast, those with healthy boundaries reported higher levels of confidence, lower stress, and a greater sense of control over their time and emotional energy.

The outcomes of their research transformed how therapists and counselors approached boundary-related issues. They discovered that learning to set limits isn't just about protecting oneself from others; it's crucial for maintaining mental health and nurturing healthier, more respectful relationships.

This research has become a cornerstone in the field of psychology, emphasizing that setting boundaries is not merely a means of self-protection but a vital component of emotional resilience and psychological health.

Exercise: Mapping Your Current Boundaries

Setting healthy boundaries is essential for creating balance and maintaining well-being in relationships. This exercise will help you reflect on the boundaries you currently have in place and identify where you may need to make improvements. Let's jump into the process step by step.

Step 1 ⟶ Select Your Relationships

Begin by considering the different types of relationships in your life. Use the following categories to guide your thinking:

- Family (parents, siblings, extended family)
- Friends
- Romantic Partners
- Work Colleagues (boss, coworkers, clients)

You may want to choose one specific relationship to focus on or work through all of them.

Step 2 ⟶ Create a Boundary Map

Take out a worksheet, table, or notebook where you can map out your boundaries. You can divide the sheet into four sections for each type of relationship or work on one at a time. Use this format as an example:

Relationship	Existing Boundaries	Where Boundaries Are Missing or Need Improvement
Family (e.g., Mother)	I limit our conversations to 20 minutes.	I need to say "no" more often to last-minute requests.
Friends (e.g., Miriam)	I avoid gossiping with her.	I need to speak up when she cancels plans without notice.
Romantic Partner	I communicate my feelings regularly.	I need to ask for more personal space after work.

Relationship	Existing Boundaries	Where Boundaries Are Missing or Need Improvement

Relationship	Existing Boundaries	Where Boundaries Are Missing or Need Improvement

Think back to a time when you felt uncomfortable or even resentful in a relationship. Maybe a friend shared too much personal information, or a family member consistently invaded your personal space.

These uncomfortable moments are often signs that your boundaries need attention. When we don't set clear boundaries, we can end up feeling overwhelmed, taken advantage of, or emotionally drained—like we're leaving the door open to anyone, regardless of how much we can actually handle.

But when we create and maintain healthy boundaries, we foster relationships built on mutual respect and understanding. Boundaries allow us to communicate our needs with confidence and also respect the limits of others. While this doesn't guarantee smooth sailing in every relationship, it gives us the tools to handle challenges with more ease and less conflict.

Think of boundaries like the perimeter of a garden. A well-kept garden has clear borders—whether fences or hedges—that protect the plants within and prevent unwanted intrusion. Just like in a garden, personal boundaries create a safe space for you to grow and flourish. They give you the security to nurture your own well-being, free from constant external pressures.

Recognizing the Impact of Unhealthy Boundaries

Unhealthy boundaries tend to show up in two main ways: as weak, porous boundaries or as rigid, inflexible ones. Both extremes can harm your relationships and well-being.

Weak boundaries are like having a flimsy fence around your yard—anyone can step over it and invade your space. This often leads to people taking advantage of your kindness or generosity, leaving you feeling resentful, overwhelmed, and emotionally drained. You might find yourself constantly giving to others, neglecting your own needs, and feeling exhausted as a result.

On the flip side, rigid boundaries are like living behind a fortress. While they may protect you from harm, they also shut people out. If you have rigid boundaries, you might struggle to open up, trust others, or ask for help. This can lead to feelings of loneliness and make it hard to form meaningful connections or maintain healthy relationships.

Unhealthy boundaries can show up differently depending on the type of relationship. In families, it might look like enmeshment, where personal and emotional boundaries blur, making it hard for individuals to function independently.

In friendships, unhealthy boundaries can lead to oversharing or codependency, where one person becomes overly reliant on the other. In romantic relationships, it might involve difficulty saying "no" or tolerating disrespectful behavior.

The consequences of weak or rigid boundaries can be far-reaching. They can fuel feelings of burnout, resentment, anxiety, or even depression. You may feel constantly depleted, struggle with low self-esteem, and have trouble asserting your own needs.

Recognizing these unhealthy patterns is the first step toward healthier boundaries. It's about understanding how your current boundaries—or lack thereof—are affecting your well-being and relationships. Acknowledging the need for change allows you to take action and start creating a life where your limits are respected and your needs are met.

How have your boundaries (or lack thereof) shaped your relationships?

____

____

____

____

What are your initial thoughts and feelings about embarking on this boundary-setting journey?

____

____

____

____

"If you don't set boundaries, you are going to end up feeling resentful." – Anne Katherine

Chapter 2

TYPES OF BOUNDARIES

ia came to my office about a year into her relationship with Jacob. She was bright, career-driven, and confident in many ways, but when it came to her relationship, she often felt small and second-guessed herself.

I could sense, even in her first session, that Mia had a vibrant energy about her—a love for life and for pursuing her passions. But there was also an underlying tension, a restlessness she couldn't shake off.

During our sessions, Mia would often talk about how much she loved Jacob, how deeply she valued their relationship, and yet, she couldn't explain why she felt so emotionally drained.

It became clear as she opened up that Jacob had a subtle way of imposing his opinions on almost every aspect of her life—from her career choices to how she should spend her free time, and even her hobbies.

What started as occasional advice from Jacob soon evolved into a pattern. Every time Mia shared something she was excited about, Jacob would have a suggestion, a comment, or, more often than not, a critique.

One particular session stands out in my memory. Mia had just been offered an exciting promotion at work, one that aligned perfectly with her long-term career goals. But when she told Jacob about it, his response was less than enthusiastic.

He questioned whether taking on more responsibility was the right move for her, given that they had been discussing marriage and potentially starting a family soon. Jacob's concerns planted seeds of doubt in Mia's mind. By the time she sat down with me, what should have been a moment of celebration had turned into a period of anxiety.

I asked Mia to reflect on how often she found herself questioning her own decisions after talking to Jacob. She hesitated for a moment, then slowly started listing all the times she had shifted her choices because of his opinions—whether it was about the projects she took on, the friends she made time for, or even how she spent her weekends.

The realization hit her hard. Mia had unknowingly allowed Jacob's thoughts and perspectives to overshadow her own, leading her to lose sight of what she truly wanted.

In therapy, we began working on the concept of mental boundaries—the idea that while it's natural to consider a partner's perspective, it's essential to maintain autonomy over your own thoughts, values, and decisions. I explained that mental boundaries allow you to keep your own voice clear, even in the midst of someone else's opinions.

Mia's journey to reclaim her mental boundaries wasn't easy. She struggled with guilt, worried that asserting herself would create distance between her and Jacob. But as we explored the importance of being true to her own desires and ambitions, Mia grew more confident in articulating her thoughts.

One of our key exercises involved writing down her goals and decisions before discussing them with Jacob. This helped her stay grounded in her convictions and gave her the strength to recognize when she was compromising her own mental space.

When Mia finally opened up to Jacob about how she felt, the conversation was difficult, but necessary.

She explained to him that while she valued his input, she needed to trust her own judgment and have the freedom to make decisions that aligned with her personal goals.

At first, Jacob was taken aback. He hadn't realized that his advice, which he had intended as supportive, was having such a negative impact. To his credit, he was willing to listen and understand. Over time, they worked together to build a healthier dynamic where Mia's autonomy was respected, and Jacob learned to provide feedback only when asked for it.

Exploring the Spectrum

Boundaries are not one-size-fits-all. They come in various forms, each serving a unique purpose in protecting our well-being and shaping how we interact with the world. Here's a look at the different types of boundaries:

Physical Boundaries

These are the most obvious and relate to our personal space and physical touch. Physical boundaries protect us from unwanted physical interactions. For instance, feeling uncomfortable when someone invades your personal space or touches you without consent highlights the need for these boundaries. They help communicate what is acceptable for our comfort and safety.

Emotional Boundaries

Emotional boundaries protect our feelings and emotional health. They set limits on how others can engage with our emotions. Imagine sharing something deeply personal, only to be met with mockery or indifference. This painful experience underscores the need for emotional boundaries, which ensure that our emotions are treated with care, respect, and validation.

Mental Boundaries

Mental boundaries safeguard our thoughts, opinions, and beliefs. They allow us to maintain intellectual autonomy without being pressured to adopt someone else's viewpoints. For example, if someone tries to force their beliefs on you or dismisses your ideas, they're crossing your mental boundaries. These boundaries help you engage in respectful conversations without compromising your beliefs.

Material Boundaries

Material boundaries relate to our possessions and resources. They define how we share or lend our belongings. If you've ever hesitated to lend something valuable or been upset when someone damaged something you loaned out, you were experiencing a breach of your material boundaries. These boundaries help protect your resources and ensure that others respect your ownership.

Time Boundaries

Time boundaries are vital for managing how we allocate our time and energy. They protect us from over-commitment and allow us to prioritize rest and self-care. For example, if you constantly feel obligated to say "yes" to every request, even when you're exhausted, it's a sign of weak time boundaries. These boundaries empower you to make deliberate choices about how you spend your time, ensuring you're not overstretched.

Digital Boundaries

In today's world, digital boundaries are becoming increasingly important. They govern how we interact with social media, email, and technology, protecting our time, attention, and mental well-being. The pressure of constant notifications, or feeling like you have to present a certain image online, illustrates the need for digital boundaries. Setting limits on screen time, online engagement, and digital availability helps you maintain a healthy balance between your online and offline life.

Understanding these different types of boundaries gives you the tools to create a life that feels balanced and aligned with your values. With clear boundaries in place, you can build healthier relationships and navigate social situations with confidence, knowing your limits are respected.

Exercise: Recognizing Your Limits

This exercise will guide you through the process of identifying your physical, emotional, and mental limits. Recognizing these limits is crucial for setting healthy boundaries and maintaining your well-being. Follow the steps below to get started.

Step 1 ⟶ Find a Quiet Space

Before diving into the exercise, find a quiet space where you can reflect without distractions. Grab a journal or a notebook to write down your thoughts.

Step 2 ⟶ Explore Your Physical Limits

Ask yourself the following questions to understand your physical boundaries. Write down your responses.

How do I feel when my body is tired or overworked?

- Describe any signs of fatigue, tension, or discomfort.

What activities drain me physically?

- List any tasks, jobs, or situations that make you feel exhausted, even when you've had enough rest.

How much rest do I need to feel physically balanced?

- Consider how much sleep, relaxation, or downtime you need to feel recharged.

What are my non-negotiables for physical well-being?

- Identify activities or habits (e.g., regular meals, exercise, sleep) that you need to maintain your health.

Step 3 ⟶ Explore Your Emotional Limits

Understanding your emotional boundaries is essential to prevent burnout and emotional overwhelm. Reflect on these questions:

What emotions do I find overwhelming or difficult to manage?

- Are there particular feelings (e.g., anger, sadness, anxiety) that make you feel emotionally exhausted?

In what situations do I tend to feel emotionally drained?

- Think about personal relationships, work environments, or social settings that leave you feeling emotionally depleted.

What behaviors from others make me uncomfortable?

- Identify actions or words from others that overstep your emotional boundaries.

How do I typically react when my emotional limits are crossed?

- Write down how you respond when you've reached your emotional limit (e.g., withdrawing, feeling irritated, or getting anxious).

Step 4 ⟶ Explore Your Mental Limits

Mental limits relate to how much cognitive load you can handle before feeling mentally overwhelmed. Use these prompts to dig deeper:

When do I feel mentally overloaded?

- List activities or tasks (e.g., multitasking, problem-solving) that make you feel mentally exhausted.

What helps me regain focus and mental clarity?

- Think of strategies you use to reset your mind (e.g., taking breaks, going for a walk, meditating).

How many tasks can I manage at once before feeling overwhelmed?

- Reflect on whether multitasking helps or hinders your mental capacity.

What boundaries do I need to maintain my mental health?

- Write down practices (e.g., setting clear work hours, limiting social media) that protect your mental well-being.

Step 5 ⟶ Be Honest with Yourself

After reflecting on your physical, emotional, and mental limits, it's time to embrace honesty. Ask yourself:

Am I currently honoring these limits, or am I pushing myself too far?

- Reflect on whether you are respecting your boundaries or ignoring them to please others.

What can I realistically handle without feeling overwhelmed?

- Write down your tolerance level in different areas of your life (e.g., work, relationships, personal time).

Step 6 ⟶ Set Boundaries Based on Your Limits

Now that you've recognized your limits, it's time to think about setting boundaries. Consider these questions:

What specific boundaries do I need to protect my physical, emotional, and mental well-being?

- Write down the boundaries you need to implement based on your limits.

How will I communicate these boundaries to others?

- Plan how you will express your needs to others in a clear and respectful way.

Step 7 ⟶ Reflect and Revisit

Your limits may change over time as you grow and face new challenges. Commit to revisiting this exercise regularly to check in with yourself.

In which areas of your life do you find it most challenging to set boundaries?

____

____

____

____

What are your typical reactions when someone oversteps your boundaries?

____

____

____

____

Chapter 3

THE ART OF SAYING NO

In 2012, a groundbreaking study on assertiveness and saying "no" was conducted by **Vanessa K. Bohns**, a social psychologist from Cornell University, and her team. The research, which focused on the social dynamics of requests and refusals, involved over 1,400 participants and sought to uncover why people struggle to decline requests, even when it may go against their interests.

The study took place across various settings, including university campuses and public spaces, and involved asking participants to make small but somewhat uncomfortable requests of strangers—such as asking them to commit acts they knew were wrong, like vandalizing a library book.

The goal was to measure how easily people would say "no" to these awkward requests. To the researchers' surprise, many participants found it incredibly hard to refuse, even though the task was clearly inappropriate. The study revealed that most people underestimate how much pressure they feel to comply and overestimate how easily they can say "no."

Bohns found that one of the key reasons people struggle to assert themselves is because they feel a greater fear of disappointing others than of compromising their own values or well-being.

This fear of social rejection often drives people to say "yes" when they really want to say "no." The research also revealed a crucial insight—those making the requests rarely realized how uncomfortable or pressured the other person felt. In fact, the "askers" often perceived the "refusers" as far more assertive than the refusers themselves believed they were being.

The outcome of the study was clear: people overestimate the negative consequences of saying no, and in doing so, they sacrifice their own needs for the sake of avoiding temporary discomfort.

The research also highlighted that with proper communication, assertiveness training, and practice, saying "no" becomes easier over time. When framed positively and respectfully, refusals are more likely to be accepted without backlash.

Saying No Without Guilt or Fear

The word no holds a strange power. It's short, simple, yet incredibly difficult for many of us to say. We twist ourselves into pretzels to avoid uttering that syllable—agreeing to things we don't want to do, attending events we'd rather skip, and taking on tasks that leave us feeling resentful. But why is it so hard to say no?

The struggle often stems from deep-seated fears and anxieties. We may be people-pleasers, terrified of disappointing others or facing their disapproval. The fear of conflict, rejection, or losing relationships can feel overwhelming, leading us to avoid confrontation at all costs. Sometimes, we fear missing out, even when the opportunity doesn't align with our true desires. This internal tug-of-war between wanting to be liked and protecting our own needs keeps us trapped in a cycle of overcommitting.

But here's the truth: saying no isn't selfish or rude—it's an act of self-respect. Every time you say no to something that drains you or doesn't serve your goals, you're essentially saying yes to something more meaningful. That yes might be to an existing commitment, much-needed rest, or an activity that truly lights you up.

Learning to say no without guilt is a crucial part of setting healthy boundaries. It's about recognizing that your needs are valid, and it's okay to prioritize them. It's about communicating your no confidently and compassionately, making space for the things that really matter.

Here are some strategies to help you overcome the no hurdle:

1. Know Your Priorities: What truly matters to you? When you're clear on your values and goals, it becomes easier to decline things that don't serve them.

2. Recognize Your Limits: Be realistic about your time, energy, and resources. You can't do everything, and that's perfectly fine.

3. Practice Assertive Communication: Clearly and respectfully express your no without apologizing or making excuses. Stand firm in your decision.

4. Offer Alternatives: If appropriate, suggest other options or compromises. For instance, "I can't make this meeting, but I'm available next week."

5. Use "I" Statements: Own your no by framing it in terms of your needs. Instead of saying, "I can't," say, "I'm already committed to something else."

6. Remember that "No" Is a Complete Sentence: You don't owe anyone a lengthy explanation. A simple no can suffice, without justifications.

Setting Limits with Different Personality Types

When setting boundaries, it's crucial to consider the personality of the person you're interacting with and adapt your approach accordingly.

Assertive individuals tend to be confident, respectful of others' opinions, and open to direct communication. With these individuals, setting boundaries can be more straightforward. You can clearly express your needs using "I" statements, such as "I need some time for myself this weekend," and offer alternatives where necessary. Assertive people often appreciate directness and are likely to respect your boundaries as long as they understand the reasoning behind them.

Passive individuals may require a gentler approach. They are often hesitant to express their own needs or may struggle with assertiveness themselves. In these cases, patience and encouragement are key. Gently explain why you're setting a boundary, and reassure them that it's about creating a healthier dynamic, not about pushing them away. For example, "I need to take a break from social events for my own well-being. It doesn't mean I don't value our time together." Reassuring them helps ensure they don't misinterpret your boundaries as rejection.

Aggressive individuals can present more of a challenge. They might resist boundaries, become defensive, or attempt to dominate the conversation. With aggressive personalities, it's essential to remain calm and assertive without becoming reactive. Firmly express your boundaries while maintaining respect, such as "I understand your perspective, but I need to stick to my decision." Avoid engaging in arguments or power struggles, as this can escalate the situation. In some cases, you may need to disengage from the conversation or involve a neutral third party if things become too heated.

Exercise: Practicing Saying "No" in Various Scenarios

This exercise is designed to help you become more comfortable with setting boundaries by practicing how to say "no" in a variety of situations. Learning to say "no" in a confident, respectful, and clear manner is a vital part of maintaining healthy boundaries.

Step 1 ⟶ **Understand the Importance of Saying "No"**

Before jumping into the exercise, remind yourself why setting boundaries is crucial. Saying "no" is about protecting your time, energy, and emotional well-being. It's not about being rude or unkind; it's about respecting your own limits.

Step 2 ⟶ **Review the Scenarios**

Below are some common scenarios where you might need to say "no." Take a moment to read through them. Imagine yourself in each situation.

Scenario 1: A colleague asks you to take on extra work when you're already overwhelmed.

Scenario 2: A friend invites you to an event, but you're exhausted and need time to recharge.

Scenario 3: A family member gives you unsolicited advice that you don't agree with or need.

Scenario 4: Someone asks to borrow money or a personal item, but you're not comfortable with it.

Step 3 ⟶ Explore Different Approaches to Saying "No"

For each scenario, practice saying "no" in a way that feels true to your personality and situation. There's no one-size-fits-all approach, so experiment with different phrases. Here are a few strategies you can try:

Direct but Polite: Clearly state your decision without over-explaining.

- Example: "I appreciate the offer, but I have to decline."

Gratitude with a Boundary: Express appreciation for the offer, but explain why you're saying no.

- Example: "Thanks for thinking of me, but I'm not available right now."

Deferring the Decision: If you're unsure or need time, it's okay to buy time to think.

- Example: "Let me check my schedule and get back to you."

Offering an Alternative: If possible, you can suggest another option or solution.

- Example: "I can't help with that, but maybe I can assist another time."

Step 4 ⟶ Practice Out Loud

Now, practice saying "no" out loud for each scenario. Use a mirror, or role-play with a friend or family member if possible. Focus on keeping your tone firm but kind, and avoid apologizing unnecessarily. Remember, you don't owe long explanations.

Step 5 ⟶ Reflect on Your Comfort Level

After practicing, reflect on which phrases or approaches felt the most comfortable for you. Did some situations feel more difficult than others? Write down your thoughts on why certain "no's" felt easier or harder to say. This can help you understand your personal boundaries better.

Step 6 ⟶ Apply it to Real Life

Finally, challenge yourself to use these "no" phrases in your everyday life. The more you practice, the easier it will become. Remember, setting boundaries is a skill that grows with time and repetition.

What fears or beliefs hold you back from saying no?

____

____

____

____

How can you say no while maintaining respect for yourself and others?

____

____

____

____

Chapter 4

PILOTING RESISTANCE AND PUSHBACK

When Rachel first came to me for therapy, I could sense a deep exhaustion in her, a weariness not just from daily life but from something heavier, more ingrained. Rachel was a high school teacher in her early 40s, independent in many ways yet burdened by an invisible weight.

As she began to open up in our sessions, she revealed the extent of her father's involvement in her life, even as a grown woman. The nature of her struggle wasn't obvious to everyone in her life, but Rachel felt her father's hold on her every day.

Rachel's father, a man with strong opinions and a belief in his ability to "rescue" her, had always tried to direct her decisions—from her career path to her choice of friends, even to where she lived.

He would criticize her relationships, often making unsolicited comments about her choices, especially regarding men he thought were "wrong" for her.

If Rachel expressed excitement about a new relationship or a personal decision, her father would respond with dismissive remarks or even warnings, framing his comments as concern but laced with judgment.

She shared one instance where, after she told him she planned to move to a new city for a teaching opportunity, he immediately responded, "You know you'll regret that. You never think these things through." Despite her confidence in her decision, Rachel found herself second-guessing herself, wondering if he was right.

Rachel's father's patterns of emotional manipulation often took a subtle form, making it difficult for her to recognize or confront. When she resisted his influence, he would often play the victim, expressing deep disappointment or giving her the silent treatment. Over time, Rachel had internalized a sense of guilt whenever she asserted her independence, questioning whether she was selfish or ungrateful for not heeding his advice.

In therapy, we began unraveling these interactions, examining the impact of his subtle control on her mental health. I encouraged Rachel to see these behaviors for what they were: attempts at emotional manipulation, driven by her father's need to maintain a sense of authority.

We worked on building her self-confidence, emphasizing her right to make independent decisions without seeking his approval.

Rachel's journey wasn't easy. At first, she struggled to set boundaries with her father, fearing his reactions and the possibility of severing their relationship. She would rehearse responses with me, preparing to stand her ground in conversations with him.

For example, if her father began criticizing a relationship or decision she'd made, Rachel practiced calmly replying, "Dad, I appreciate your concern, but this is my choice, and I need you to respect it." Her father initially responded with guilt-laden comments like, "You've changed, Rachel. You don't care about my opinion anymore." Each time, she braced herself against the familiar pangs of guilt, reminding herself that she deserved the freedom to live life on her terms.

Over the months, Rachel's confidence grew. She didn't need her father's approval as she once had, and her anxiety in his presence gradually lessened. Their relationship didn't change overnight, but Rachel's newfound boundary-setting skills allowed her to interact with him from a place of strength rather than submission. She saw that maintaining boundaries didn't mean severing ties; rather, it allowed her to approach the relationship with more clarity and self-respect.

Responding to Challenges and Objections

Setting boundaries is rarely a smooth, effortless process. Even when approached with care and respect, new boundaries may be met with resistance, objections, or even attempts to manipulate you back into old patterns. Being prepared for these challenges—and equipped with strategies to respond effectively—will help you stay grounded and assertive.

Imagine you finally gather the courage to tell a friend that you won't be available to help them with errands every weekend. You explain that, while you value the friendship, you need more time for yourself. Instead of understanding, your friend begins guilt-tripping you with statements like, "I thought you were my friend. Real friends always help each other out. I guess I can't count on you anymore."

In such moments, it's easy to feel flustered, defensive, or pressured to give in. However, it's crucial to remember that your boundaries are valid, and you have the right to prioritize your needs. Responding calmly and assertively can help you stay true to your boundaries while maintaining respectful communication.

Strategies to Handle Objections and Guilt Trips

1. **Reiterate Your Boundary:** Use clear, concise language to restate your boundary without apologizing or making excuses. A simple, direct response reinforces your commitment to this change.

2. **Acknowledge Their Feelings:** Show empathy for their perspective, even if you don't agree with it. For instance, you might say, "I understand that you're disappointed, but this is something I need to do for myself." Empathy can help diffuse tension without undermining your boundary.

3. **Stand Your Ground:** Remain confident in your decision. Avoid getting swayed by guilt trips or emotional appeals, and remind yourself why you set this boundary. This strengthens your resolve and communicates that your boundaries are important.

4. **Offer Alternatives:** If appropriate, suggest alternative solutions that respect both your needs and theirs. For example, "I'm available to chat or catch up on weekdays but need weekends for myself." Offering alternatives shows you still care without compromising your limits.

5. **Set Consequences if Needed**: If they continue to push, be prepared to set consequences for further pressure. You might say, "If you keep bringing this up, I'll need to step back from this conversation for a while." Consequences reinforce that your boundaries are non-negotiable.

Phrases for Calm, Assertive Responses

To help you maintain a firm but respectful tone, here are some scripts for reiterating boundaries without becoming defensive:

- *"I understand how you feel, but my decision is final."*
- *"I'm happy to discuss this further, but I won't be changing my mind."*
- *"I value our relationship, and I need you to respect my boundaries."*
- *"I'm not willing to compromise on this."*
- *"I'm happy to help in other ways, but not with this particular request."*

Setting boundaries isn't about "winning" a conversation or proving a point—it's about creating healthier, more respectful relationships. By responding to challenges with calmness and assertiveness, you show others that your needs and boundaries are valuable, while also encouraging a foundation of mutual respect. Over time, this can strengthen your relationships and help you cultivate a life that honors your own well-being.

Maintaining Boundaries with Difficult People

Setting boundaries with difficult people—those who are manipulative, narcissistic, or habitually complaining—can be especially challenging. These individuals often know how to push your buttons, guilt-trip you, or play the victim, making it feel like maintaining your limits is a constant battle. However, even with challenging personalities, it's essential to assert your right to set boundaries and protect your well-being.

Imagine you have a coworker who frequently offloads their work onto you at the last minute. Each time you bring it up, they have a ready excuse or subtly guilt-trip you into feeling responsible. You're frustrated but also concerned about stirring up conflict or risking your job.

Maintaining boundaries with difficult people requires vigilance, consistency, and resilience. It's about establishing firm limits, communicating them assertively, and holding to your stance, even in the face of pushback. Here are some strategies to help navigate boundaries with challenging individuals:

Be Direct and Unambiguous

Avoid giving hints or speaking indirectly. State your boundaries clearly and assertively, leaving no room for misinterpretation. For instance, tell your coworker, "I won't be able to take on last-minute tasks anymore. Please let me know in advance if you need help."

Document Everything

In a professional or legal context, it's wise to keep records of all relevant interactions. Document agreements, boundary violations, and any conversations where you communicated your boundaries. This not only provides you with concrete evidence if needed but also reinforces your commitment to upholding your boundaries.

Don't Engage in Arguments

Difficult individuals may try to argue, blame, or create power struggles. Resist the urge to debate or defend yourself. Calmly reiterate your boundary, and if necessary, politely disengage. For example, say, "I understand your perspective, but my decision stands."

4. Set Consequences and Follow Through

Determine clear consequences for boundary violations, and be prepared to enforce them. Depending on the situation, this might mean reducing contact, reconsidering the relationship, or taking formal action if necessary. If the coworker continues to offload tasks despite your boundary, you might say, "If this continues, I'll need to speak with our supervisor about workload expectations."

Seek Support

Handling difficult personalities can be draining. Seek advice and support from trusted friends, family, or a therapist. Having a support system reinforces your confidence, helps validate your experiences, and reminds you that you're not alone in managing these challenges.

Be Consistent and Stand Your Ground

Difficult individuals often test boundaries, hoping that persistence will make you relent. Stick to your boundaries every time they're challenged, even if it means repeating yourself or setting additional limits. Consistency reinforces the message that you won't bend, regardless of pressure or manipulation.

You can't change other people's behavior, but you can control your responses and enforce your boundaries. Dealing with difficult individuals may require additional resolve, but protecting your well-being and maintaining healthy, respectful relationships is worth the effort. By staying firm in your boundaries, you create space for a more fulfilling and peaceful life, free from manipulation and resentment.

Exercise: Boundary Toolkit

Step 1 ⟶ Identify Challenging Situations

- Reflect on past experiences where setting boundaries was difficult. Think of common scenarios where your boundaries were pushed, ignored, or misunderstood.
- Write down 3-5 specific situations (e.g., handling a demanding friend, managing work requests after hours, or dealing with family expectations). Identifying these helps clarify where your toolkit will be most useful.

Step 2 ⟶ Choose Your "Go-To" Affirmations

- Create affirmations that reinforce your right to set boundaries. Affirmations like "I deserve to protect my energy," or "It's okay to say no without feeling guilty" are helpful reminders.
- Select a few affirmations that resonate most with you. Write them in your toolkit to revisit when facing a boundary challenge. These affirmations should boost your confidence and reduce self-doubt.

Step 3 ⟶ Add Relaxation Techniques

- Pick relaxation techniques that can calm you quickly in high-stress moments. Options might include deep breathing, grounding exercises, or a short walk.

- Practice these techniques when you're calm to get comfortable using them. Make a list of 2-3 techniques you find most effective and add them to your toolkit.

Step 4 ———→ Identify Supportive People

- List supportive people in your life who encourage and respect your boundaries, such as friends, family members, or mentors.
- Keep their contact info handy in your toolkit. Knowing you have people you can reach out to in difficult situations can make enforcing boundaries easier and provide emotional support when needed.

Step 5 ———→ Personalize and Carry Your Toolkit

- Write down or create a physical or digital version of your toolkit. You might keep it in a notebook, a phone app, or a small card for quick access.
- Review and update your toolkit regularly. As new boundary challenges arise, add new affirmations, techniques, or supportive individuals to keep your toolkit relevant and helpful.

How do you typically react when faced with resistance to your boundaries?

____

____

____

____

What coping mechanisms can you employ when feeling uncomfortable setting boundaries?

____

____

____

____

"Boundaries are a part of self-care. They are healthy, normal, and necessary." – Doreen Virtue

Chapter 5

BOUNDARIES IN RELATIONSHIPS

Dr. Karen Kayser, a well-respected psychiatrist, conducted her pivotal research in the early 1990s, focusing on boundary setting in family and romantic relationships.

Her study, conducted at Boston University, closely examined married couples navigating issues of control, autonomy, and respect in their relationships. Kayser's research aimed to explore how boundaries—or the lack of them—affect the quality and longevity of intimate relationships.

In her study, Kayser analyzed couples experiencing various levels of satisfaction, interviewing each partner about their perception of decision-making in the relationship.

One key focus was to understand how unilateral decisions (decisions made by one partner without the other's input) impacted relationship health.

She found that in relationships where one partner consistently overstepped the other's boundaries—exerting control by ignoring or invalidating their partner's input—the result was a significant decline in relationship satisfaction.

One key focus was to understand how unilateral decisions (decisions made by one partner without the other's input) impacted relationship health. She found that in relationships where one partner consistently overstepped the other's boundaries—exerting control by ignoring or invalidating their partner's input—the result was a significant decline in relationship satisfaction.

Many of these couples reported feelings of resentment, disconnection, and an overall lack of intimacy.

Kayser's findings were clear: boundaries in relationships are crucial for maintaining mutual respect and emotional closeness. When both partners feel their voices are heard and their autonomy respected, their relationships are more resilient and satisfying.

This concept isn't limited to romantic partnerships—it extends to family relationships, where adult children, parents, and siblings benefit from establishing and respecting boundaries to foster healthy connections.

In practical terms, Kayser's study highlights that boundaries empower individuals to express their needs, enabling healthier interactions within close relationships. By setting and honoring boundaries, partners create a space where both people feel valued, resulting in a relationship built on equality, empathy, and understanding.

Setting Healthy Limits with Family, Friends, and Partners

Setting boundaries in relationships can be challenging, especially when navigating emotional dynamics with family, friends, or romantic partners. But healthy boundaries are essential for maintaining your identity, honoring your needs, and fostering respectful communication.

Imagine your parents expect financial help, your friend sees you as their on-call therapist, and your partner continually pressures you to attend their family events when you'd rather recharge at home. These scenarios are classic boundary challenges, each needing a unique approach.

With Family

Family relationships often carry complex expectations and feelings of guilt, which can make setting boundaries difficult. However, boundaries with family might involve saying no to excessive favors, deciding what personal information you share, or establishing clear expectations around visits or communication.

For example:

"Mom, Dad, I love you, but I need to prioritize my own financial stability right now. I can't afford to lend money at this time, but I'm here to support you in other ways."

With Friends

Friendships are grounded in mutual respect and support. Sometimes, setting boundaries with friends means saying no to overextending yourself, sharing your discomfort with certain conversations, or clarifying how much emotional support you're able to give.

For example:

"I care about you, and I want to support you, but I'm not equipped to help with relationship advice right now. Talking to a therapist might give you more insight and support."

With Romantic Partners

In romantic relationships, boundaries create a balance between intimacy and independence. Setting boundaries with a partner might mean voicing your need for personal time, expressing your comfort levels around intimacy, or clarifying how finances and decisions are managed in the relationship.

For example:

"I love spending time with you, but I also need some time to recharge. Would you be okay with us designating one night each week to do our own thing?"

Creating a Culture of Respect and Understanding

Boundaries are not about creating distance; they're about fostering a healthy environment of respect and understanding in relationships. They allow you to communicate your needs openly, honor your well-being, and build mutual trust and appreciation.

Imagine a relationship where both people feel at ease expressing their thoughts, feelings, and limits without fear of judgment. This is what healthy boundaries can achieve.

When respected, boundaries build a foundation of trust, open communication, and constructive conflict resolution. They enable a balance between personal individuality and a meaningful connection, allowing each person to stay true to themselves within the relationship.

To foster a culture of respect and understanding, both people must commit to open communication, empathy, and compromise. It's about recognizing that each person has their own needs and that these deserve to be respected. Here are some practical ways to build this culture:

- Practice Active Listening: Give your full attention to what the other person is saying, both verbally and through body language. Reflect back on what they're expressing to show you understand their perspective.
- Communicate Clearly and Assertively: Use "I" statements to express your needs and boundaries directly, without placing blame. Clear and respectful communication helps prevent misunderstandings.
- Be Open to Compromise: Seek solutions that respect both your needs and the other person's. Compromise can bridge differences while showing mutual consideration.
- Respect Individuality: Acknowledge that each person has their unique thoughts, feelings, and preferences. Embracing differences rather than expecting sameness allows room for growth and connection.
- Show Appreciation: Acknowledge and express gratitude for the other person's respect and effort in honoring boundaries. A little appreciation goes a long way in reinforcing positive interactions.

Creating a culture of respect and understanding is a continual effort that pays off by allowing your relationship to thrive. When boundaries are honored, relationships become a source of strength, connection, and enrichment, supporting each person in becoming their best self.

Exercise: Defining Expectations in Your Relationships

Step 1   ⟶   Identify the Relationships

- Make a List: Start by listing the key relationships in your life. These may include family members, friends, romantic partners, colleagues, or acquaintances.
- Consider Importance: Reflect on which relationships are most significant to you and warrant a deeper understanding of your expectations.

Step 2   ⟶   Reflect on Each Relationship

Allocate Time: Set aside some quiet time to think about each relationship individually. This is crucial for understanding your feelings and expectations.

Ask Yourself: For each relationship, consider questions like:
- What role does this person play in my life?
- How do I feel when I'm with them?
- What do I appreciate about this relationship?

Step 3 ⟶ Define Your Expectations

Be Specific: For each relationship, write down your expectations. Think about your needs and desires in terms of:

- Communication: How often do you want to communicate? What mode (texts, calls, face-to-face) do you prefer?
- Support: What kind of emotional, physical, or practical support do you expect?
- Boundaries: Are there certain topics or behaviors that are off-limits for you?

Step 4 ⟶ Prioritize Your Expectations

- Rank Your Needs: After listing your expectations, prioritize them. Which are the most important to you? This will help you focus on what truly matters.
- Consider Feasibility: Reflect on whether your expectations are realistic and achievable within the context of each relationship.

Step 5 ⟶ Communicate Your Expectations

- Choose the Right Time: Find an appropriate moment to discuss your expectations with the other person. Ensure both of you are in a good emotional space for this conversation.
- Invite Feedback: Encourage the other person to share their thoughts and feelings about your expectations. This dialogue can help create mutual understanding.

Step 6 ⟶ **Reassess Regularly**

- Check-In Periodically: Relationships evolve, and so do expectations. Set reminders to revisit your expectations regularly (e.g., every few months) and adjust them as necessary.
- Stay Flexible: Be open to adjusting your expectations based on changes in the relationship or the other person's circumstances.

Step 7 ⟶ **Reflect on the Outcomes**

- Journal Your Thoughts: After discussing your expectations, take some time to reflect on how the conversation went. Write about your feelings and any changes in the relationship.
- Evaluate Your Boundaries: Consider whether your boundaries were respected and how the other person responded. This reflection can inform future boundary-setting efforts.

How can boundaries enhance your relationships?

____

____

____

____

What boundaries are essential for maintaining healthy connections?

____

____

____

____

"When you say yes to others, make sure you are not saying no to yourself." – Paulo Coelhoa

Chapter 6

BOUNDARIES AT WORK AND IN SOCIAL SETTINGS

Emma came to see me initially for stress-related concerns. A dedicated project manager in her mid-30s, she often described herself as "always on," a description that seemed more like a badge of exhaustion than pride.

She'd arrive at sessions with tension in her shoulders and circles under her eyes, apologizing if she'd missed an appointment reminder or replying late to one of my emails. Emma's entire professional life had grown around the demands of her work, where setting boundaries felt like a foreign concept, even as her well-being suffered.

As she opened up, Emma shared that her boss regularly assigned work close to the end of the day, expecting it by morning. These late-night projects had become routine, to the point where her evenings, weekends, and even vacation days were interrupted by last-minute requests.

Emma was proud of her work ethic but felt trapped, torn between wanting to be reliable and needing time for herself. The relentless cycle of overwork left her physically drained, emotionally fragile, and questioning her own boundaries.

In our sessions, Emma would sometimes express resentment but then quickly excuse her boss's behavior, attributing it to his "busy schedule" or the company's high-pressure environment.

It became clear that a pattern of people-pleasing was deeply embedded in her approach to work, making it hard for her to say "no" without guilt. I encouraged her to think about what it would look like to set some small limits, like only responding to emails until a certain time in the evening.

Gradually, Emma began to recognize her needs were valid and that healthy boundaries didn't equate to being a "bad employee." We worked on reframing her thinking, so she could see boundaries as a way to preserve her well-being rather than as a sign of weakness or failure.

I suggested she start by experimenting with a simple change: proposing a weekly check-in with her boss to review and prioritize tasks so that any last-minute surprises could be minimized.

The first time Emma tried to voice her need for limits, she felt a surge of anxiety and even texted me afterward, feeling as if she had "betrayed" her boss. But when she expressed to him that working late into the night was affecting her productivity, he was surprisingly understanding. He agreed to the weekly check-in, and Emma gradually reduced her after-hours workload.

Work and social environments often challenge our boundaries, whether it's a colleague expecting 24/7 availability or an acquaintance prying into personal matters. Boundaries in these settings are essential to safeguard our time, well-being, and privacy.

In the workplace, colleagues may overstep professional boundaries, expecting immediate responses even after hours. It's common to feel obligated to respond to these demands to appear dedicated, but this can quickly lead to burnout.

A personal example: when a colleague persistently messaged me late at night expecting a quick reply, it began to disrupt my personal time and rest. Eventually, I set a boundary by letting them know I wouldn't be checking messages after work hours, but I'd respond promptly the next morning. While there was initial resistance, they ultimately respected my boundary, and my evenings became more peaceful.

In social settings, boundaries are equally important. Overly inquisitive acquaintances sometimes feel entitled to ask personal questions that can make us uncomfortable. In these moments, I've learned the value of polite but firm redirection. By changing the subject or gently deflecting, I maintain my comfort and privacy without seeming rude or dismissive. Boundaries here are about asserting control over what I choose to share and with whom.

Setting boundaries in work and social contexts means establishing clear expectations. Assertive and respectful communication is key, whether that's declining requests for extra work, gracefully ending uncomfortable conversations, or managing your social media availability. These boundaries help cultivate respect, prevent overreach, and allow you to focus on what truly matters to you.

Establishing Professional Limits and Expectations

Imagine finally sinking into your evening, ready to unwind, when suddenly, your work phone pings.

A colleague is asking for a "quick favor" that quickly turns into an hour-long task.

Your personal time is slipping away, leaving you stressed, resentful, and mentally drained. Work-life balance feels like a distant concept, replaced by the demands of an "always-on" work culture.

Setting boundaries at work is essential to protect your well-being, manage productivity, and build respectful relationships. Clear limits allow you to recharge and prevent burnout, enabling you to bring your best self to work each day.

Here are some practical examples of workplace boundaries:

- **Managing Workload:** Realistically assessing your capacity can prevent overwhelm and ensure quality in your work. Politely declining additional tasks shows responsibility, not weakness. For instance, you might say, "I'm dedicated to delivering high-quality work, but my current workload is full. Could we prioritize my existing tasks before adding more?"

- **Declining After-Hours Requests:** Safeguarding your personal time is crucial for recharging. Declining late-night emails or calls with clarity and firmness can preserve your evenings. Consider saying, "I'm unavailable after work hours, but I'm happy to address this first thing tomorrow."
- **Handling Difficult Colleagues:** Some colleagues may not respect boundaries, interrupting, gossiping, or making inappropriate comments. Addressing these behaviors calmly and assertively can protect your focus and comfort at work. For example, try saying, "I'm focusing on a project right now. Could we catch up on this later?"

Setting boundaries at work isn't about being uncooperative; it's about fostering a healthier, more productive environment. Communicating your needs respectfully creates mutual understanding, helping you protect your time and energy while showing respect for your colleagues' needs.

Piloting Social Media and Technology with Intention

Social media and technology are designed to keep us connected and informed, but they can easily lead to distraction, comparison, and even tech-induced anxiety. Imagine scrolling through your feed, seeing carefully curated snapshots of others' lives that make yours feel less exciting, or feeling the pressure to respond instantly to every ping. These habits can drain your energy and time, leaving you less present in your real life.

Setting digital boundaries helps you regain control of how technology impacts your life. It's about making conscious choices that align with your well-being, allowing you to use digital tools in ways that enhance your life instead of detracting from it.

Here are effective strategies for setting digital boundaries:

- **Limit Screen Time:** Designate specific times to check social media or emails and use apps or phone settings to track and reduce your screen time. For example, you might limit yourself to checking social media for 15 minutes in the morning and evening.

- **Manage Notifications:** Turn off non-essential notifications to avoid constant disruptions. Set aside designated times to check messages and emails rather than reacting immediately to every alert.

- **Curate Your Feed:** Unfollow or mute accounts that trigger negative feelings or comparisons, and instead fill your feed with content that brings you joy, inspiration, or education.
- **Create Tech-Free Zones:** Designate certain times or spaces, like the dining table or your bedroom, as tech-free zones. This encourages more mindful connection with those around you and helps establish a clear boundary between online and offline life.
- **Practice Mindful Technology Use:** When you're online, stay aware and intentional. Avoid mindless scrolling or multitasking, and engage with content that's truly meaningful or beneficial to you.

Setting digital boundaries isn't about cutting off technology but rather about enhancing your relationship with it. By setting these limits, you can protect your mental health, prioritize meaningful connections, and make space for a more balanced, fulfilling life.

Exercise: Setting Boundaries for Work-Life Balance

Step 1 ⟶ **Assess Your Current Work-Life Boundaries**

Activity: Reflect on your current boundary-setting practices by asking yourself:

- Do I find it challenging to disconnect from work?
- How often do I respond to work messages or emails after hours?
- How frequently does work interfere with personal plans or activities?

Outcome: Gain awareness of the areas where your boundaries need strengthening.

Step 2 ⟶ **Reflect on Each Relationship**

Activity: Identify essential personal time that should be free from work interruptions (e.g., evenings, weekends, family time, exercise).

- Make a list of your "non-negotiables" for personal time.
- Consider what needs to be in place for you to feel refreshed and balanced.

Outcome: A clear list of times or activities you're committed to protecting as personal time.

Step 3 ⟶ **Set Up Work Communication Guidelines**

Activity: Establish rules for responding to work-related communication after hours:

- Decide on a specific "cut-off time" each evening to stop checking emails or work messages.
- Choose tools, like setting an "Out of Office" reply for certain times, or silencing work apps.
- If necessary, share your communication preferences with colleagues and supervisors (e.g., "I respond to emails from 8 a.m. to 6 p.m. Monday through Friday.").

Outcome: A concrete plan for handling after-hours communication.

Step 4 ⟶ **Communicate Your Boundaries Clearly**

Activity: Practice assertive communication by letting relevant people know about your new boundaries:

- Politely inform supervisors and team members of your availability.
- For instance, say: "I am working to maintain a healthy work-life balance, so I won't be available after 6 p.m."

Outcome: Ensures that others understand and can respect your boundaries.

Step 5 ⟶ **Prioritize and Schedule Personal Time**

Activity: Plan personal activities that matter to you and schedule them as you would a work meeting.

- Set aside specific time blocks for hobbies, family, exercise, and relaxation.
- Protect these time blocks as you would any other commitment.

Outcome: A calendar that reflects a balance between work and personal life.

Step 6 ⟶ **Practice Saying "No" When Needed**

Activity: Prepare yourself to decline additional work tasks that interfere with personal time.

- Practice responses like: "I can address this first thing in the morning" or "I've committed to a personal engagement this evening."

Outcome: Builds confidence in prioritizing your well-being over non-urgent work demands.

Step 7 ⟶ **Review and Adjust Regularly**

Activity: Check in with yourself periodically to see how well your boundaries are working.

- Ask: Are my boundaries reducing stress and enhancing my personal life? Do I need to adjust them?

How can boundaries reduce stress and prevent burnout?

____

____

____

____

What digital boundaries can you implement for a healthier relationship with technology?

____

____

____

____

Chapter 1

SELF-CARE AND BOUNDARIES

In 2018, researchers from the University of California, Berkeley, led by **Dr. Teresa Evans**, carried out a large-scale study focusing on boundaries and mental health among graduate students and early-career researchers across various fields, especially in high-stress, demanding environments.

Conducted with over 2,200 participants, this research sought to understand the emotional toll of academic pressures and the role boundaries could play in alleviating it.

The team gathered responses about mental health, burnout, and the impact of lacking boundaries between work and personal time. Results revealed that approximately 75% of participants experienced regular stress, 50% reported being overwhelmed, and nearly 40% faced severe exhaustion. Interestingly, those who had established intentional boundaries, like taking breaks for exercise, setting "off-hours" from work emails, and prioritizing sleep, reported much lower levels of anxiety and depression.

This study concluded that boundaries aren't just protective measures but essential for long-term career sustainability and well-being. Participants who dedicated time to personal needs saw benefits like improved productivity, greater satisfaction, and more robust mental health. Dr. Evans noted that setting personal boundaries allowed these students to reconnect with why they had entered their fields in the first place—preserving their passion by preventing burnout.

By applying these findings to any setting where stress and high demands exist, this research underscores the importance of boundary-setting as a form of self-care, helping individuals maintain their well-being while remaining effective and fulfilled in their careers.

Prioritizing Your Well-being and Needs

Think of your well-being as a garden. For it to thrive, it needs regular care—watering, weeding, and a solid fence to keep out anything that could cause harm. Self-care is the tending, while boundaries act as the protective fence. Both are essential, each one supporting the other, creating a flourishing inner landscape.

I used to neglect this "garden" of mine, constantly prioritizing everyone else's needs and overcommitting. I'd stretch myself thin, leaving no time or energy for my own well-being. Eventually, burnout crept in, along with feelings of resentment. Realizing I had to make a change, I started setting boundaries—not just for others but for myself.

These boundaries allowed me to say no to demands that didn't serve me, create time for what I loved, and communicate my limits clearly. By protecting my time and energy,

I could make space for self-care practices to take root and flourish. Morning walks became a peaceful routine, quiet evenings with a book felt like gifts to myself, and saying no to draining commitments was no longer a burden.

These self-care practices strengthened my boundaries, making it easier to uphold them with confidence and without guilt. The more I nurtured myself, the more resilient I became, and the better I could manage my commitments.

Self-care is not a luxury—it's essential. It's the foundation of a healthy, fulfilling life, and boundaries are the tools that protect that foundation. Together, they enable us to thrive, ensuring that our well-being remains a priority.

Cultivating Self-Respect Through Boundaries

Self-respect is like an inner compass that keeps us grounded in our own worth. It's that quiet, persistent reminder that our needs matter, our feelings matter, and our well-being matters. Boundaries are the tangible expression of that belief, the way we show the world—and ourselves—that we're committed to honoring our value.

For a long time, I struggled with self-doubt and people-pleasing, often compromising my needs to avoid conflict or gain approval. Yet, underneath it all, there was a lingering dissatisfaction, a sense that I was betraying myself. It wasn't until I started setting boundaries that I began to genuinely nurture self-respect.

Each time I declined a request that didn't sit right, each time I spoke up about my limits calmly and clearly, I felt empowered. I was showing myself that I valued my well-being enough to protect it. It was like saying, "I care enough about myself to honor my needs."

Boundaries are an act of self-love. They're how we honor our own limits, communicate our needs, and cultivate relationships that affirm our self-worth.

By setting boundaries, we're declaring, "I deserve respect, I deserve to have my needs met, and I deserve a life that feels true to me."

This commitment to self-respect builds our confidence and sense of agency, allowing us to navigate life with purpose and clarity. When we respect ourselves, we naturally attract relationships that reflect and uphold that respect.

Building self-respect through boundaries is a journey, not a single act. It's about consistently choosing to prioritize our well-being, assertively express our needs, and shape relationships that honor our inherent worth. With each boundary set, we're nurturing a deeper, more resilient sense of self-respect.

Exercise: Creating a Personalized Self-Care Plan

Step 1 ⟶ Reflect on Your Needs

- Take a moment to think about what self-care means to you. Consider your physical, emotional, and mental health. What do you feel you need most right now?
- Write down your thoughts. Use prompts like: "I feel my best when…" or "I need more of…" This reflection will help you identify areas to focus on in your self-care plan.

Step 2 ⟶ Identify Nourishing Activities

List activities that nourish you. Think about what makes you feel rejuvenated or fulfilled.

- Physical Health: Exercise, yoga, hiking, dancing, or any form of physical activity.
- Emotional Health: Journaling, connecting with friends, or practicing gratitude.
- Mental Health: Reading, meditation, or engaging in creative pursuits.

Prioritize joy and relaxation. Ensure that these activities are not just chores but are things you genuinely enjoy.

Step 3 ⟶ Set Realistic Goals

- Determine how often you can engage in self-care. Be realistic about your schedule and commitments. Aim for activities you can incorporate into your daily or weekly routine.
- Create specific goals. For example, "I will practice yoga twice a week" or "I will spend 30 minutes reading every day."

Step 4 ⟶ Schedule Your Self-Care

- Block out time in your calendar. Treat your self-care activities as appointments that cannot be missed. This prioritization reinforces the importance of self-care.
- Be specific with your scheduling. Write down the day and time for each activity. For instance, "Every Saturday at 10 AM, I will go for a walk in the park."

Step 5 ⟶ Create a Self-Care Menu

Design a self-care menu. Organize your activities into categories based on your needs:

- Quick Fixes: Activities you can do in under 15 minutes (e.g., deep breathing, quick stretches).
- Weekly Treats: Longer activities that require more time (e.g., a spa day, a longer hike).
- Monthly Goals: Larger goals that might require planning (e.g., a weekend getaway, a new class).

Step 6 ⟶ Evaluate and Adjust

- Check in with yourself regularly. After a month, reflect on how well your self-care plan is working. Are you feeling more balanced and energized?
- Make adjustments as needed. If certain activities aren't fulfilling, replace them with others that might resonate better with you.

Step 7 ⟶ Seek Support

- Share your self-care goals with someone you trust. This could be a friend, family member, or therapist. They can provide encouragement and accountability.
- Consider joining a group or community. Engaging with others who prioritize self-care can inspire you and provide new ideas.

How can boundaries support your self-care practices?

____

____

____

____

____

What are your ongoing commitments to maintaining healthy boundaries?

____

____

____

____

____

Thank You!

I want to express my heartfelt gratitude for joining me on this journey. Your openness to explore and heal with the "Effective Boundary Setting Workbook" truly means everything to me.

If you found this book valuable, I would be so grateful if you could leave a review on Amazon or wherever you bought it. Your feedback is incredibly important, both to me and to other readers. As a little thank-you, don't forget to scan the QR code for a special bonus gift.

With all my appreciation,

Isabella Cruz